ANTIQUE BIRD ART IV
FOR ADULT COLORISTS
BY CAROL MENNIG

25 ANTIQUE BIRD PRINT DESIGNS FROM 1788 TO 1936

FEATURED ARTISTS ARE:
JOHN PRIDEAUX SELBY
ROBERT MORRIS
FERN BISEL PEAT

ALPINE SWIFT

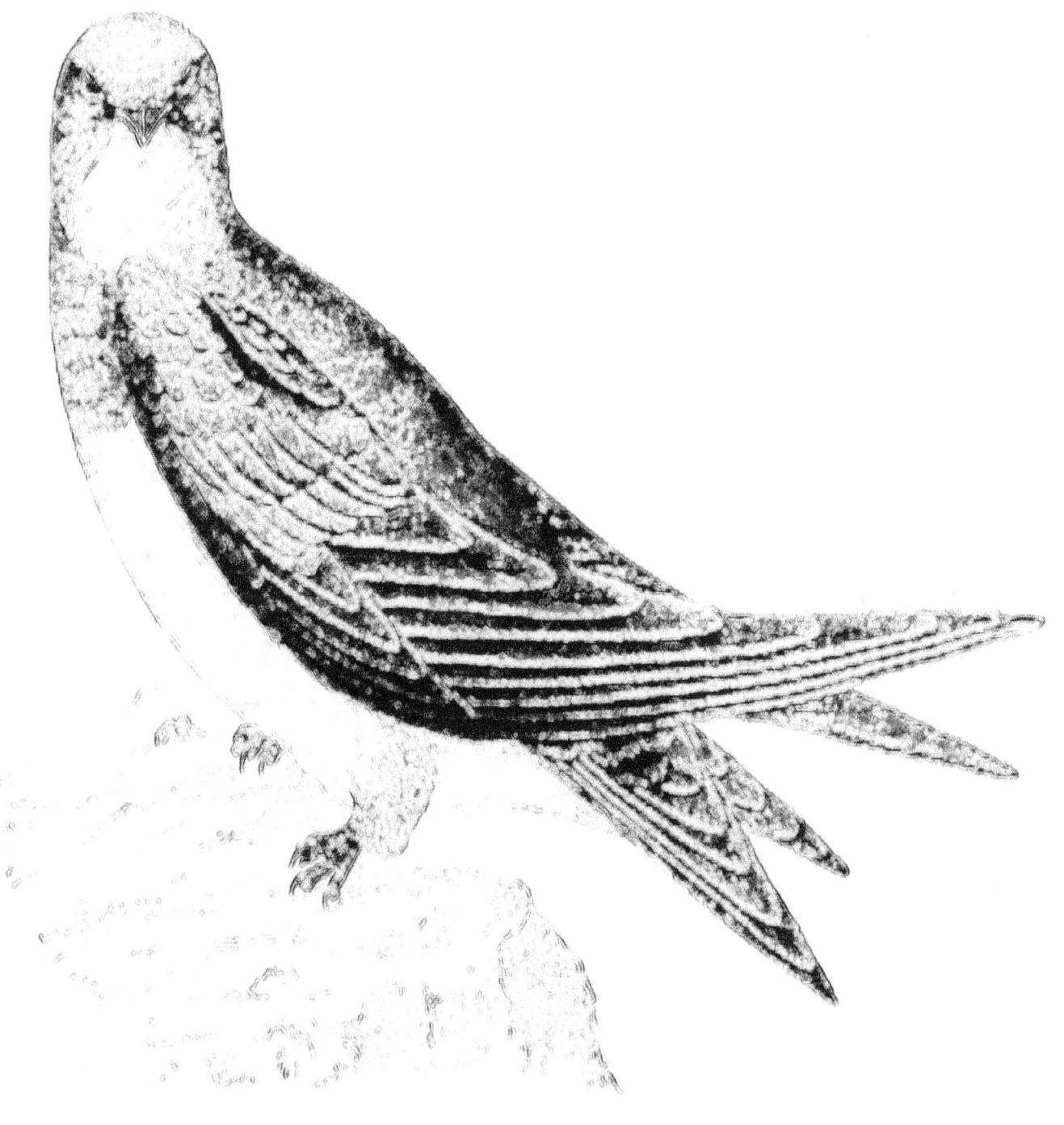

AMERICAN WHITE WINGED CROSSBILL

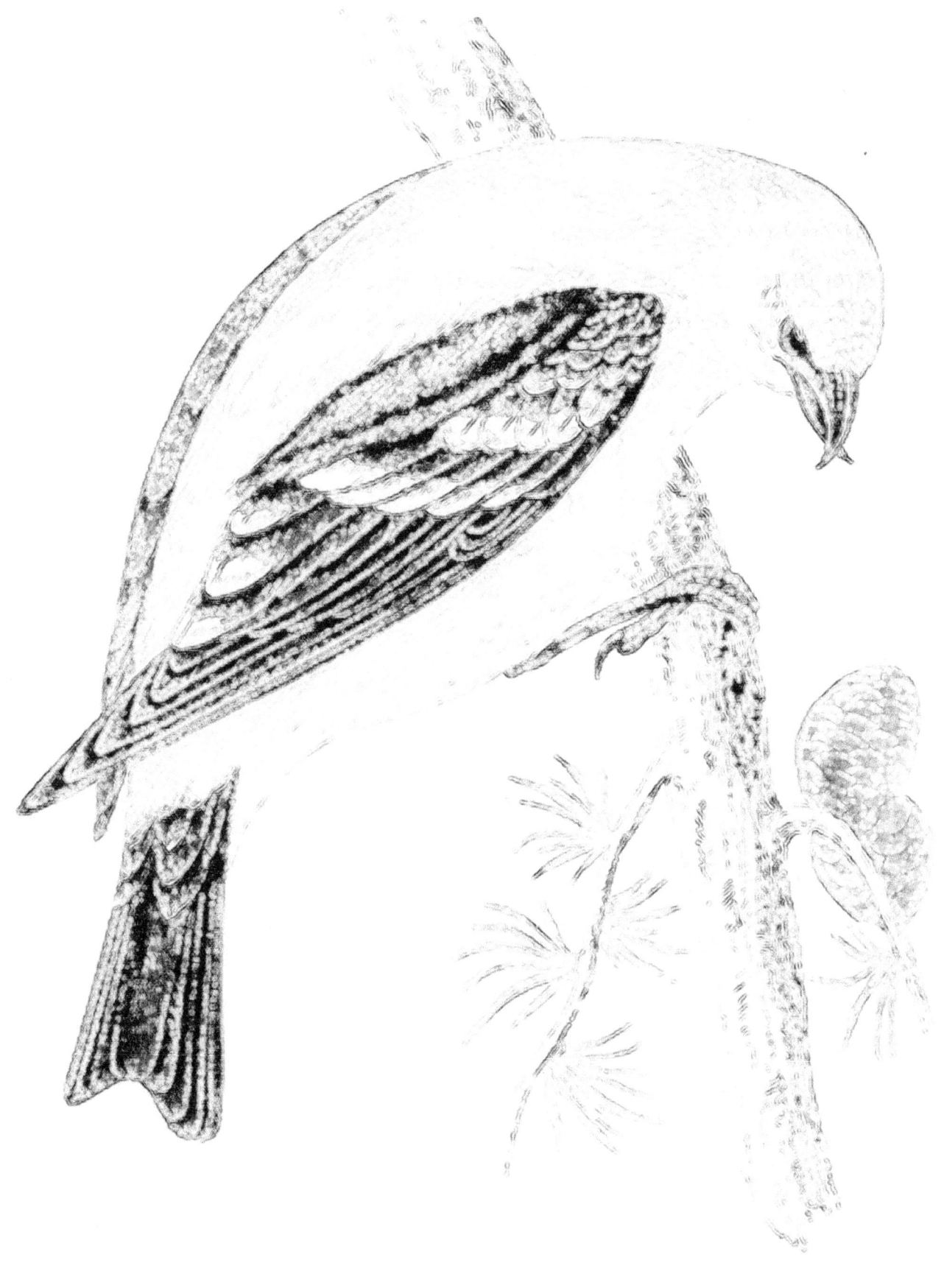

AMERICAN WIGEON

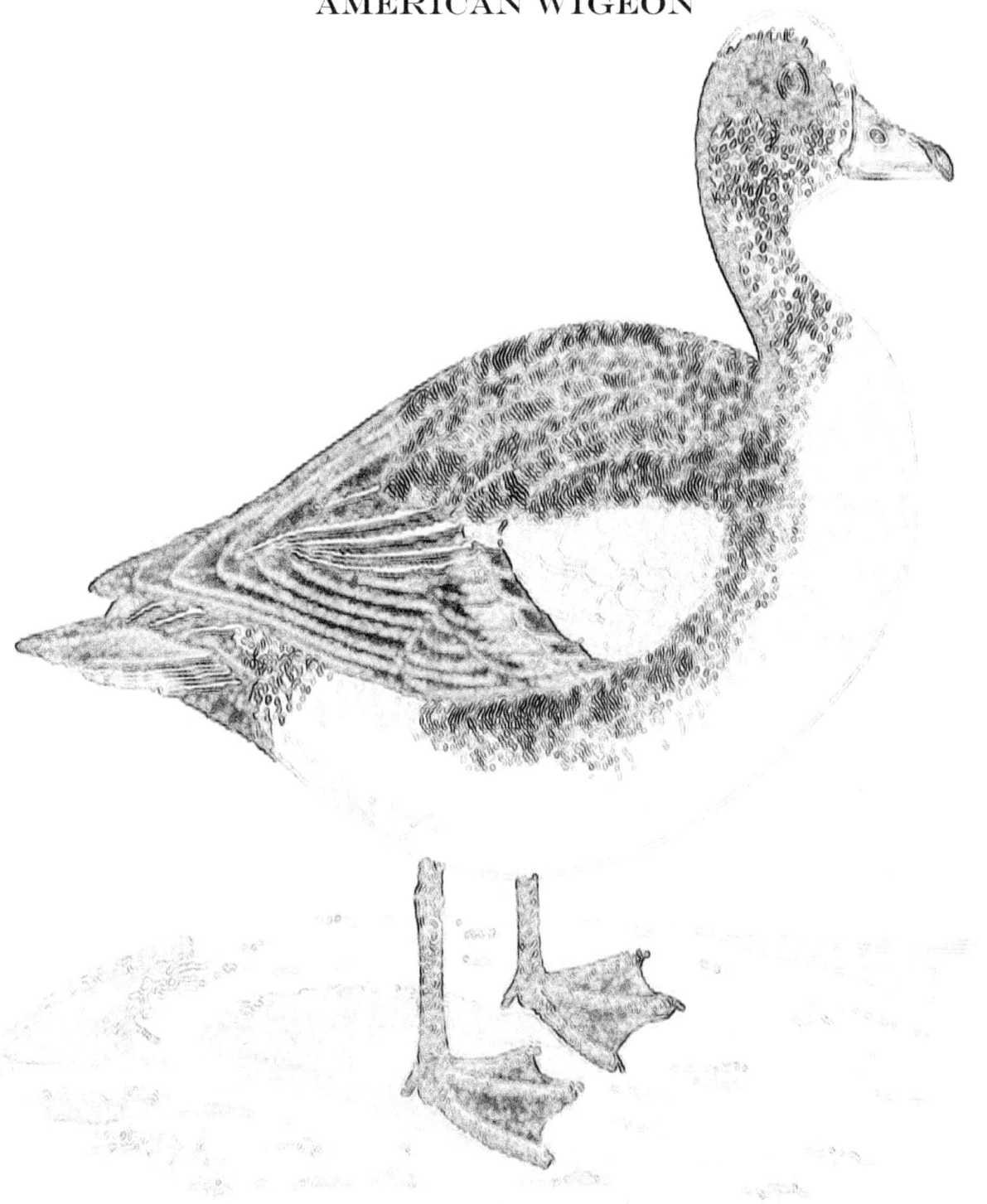

ANDALUSIAN QUAIL

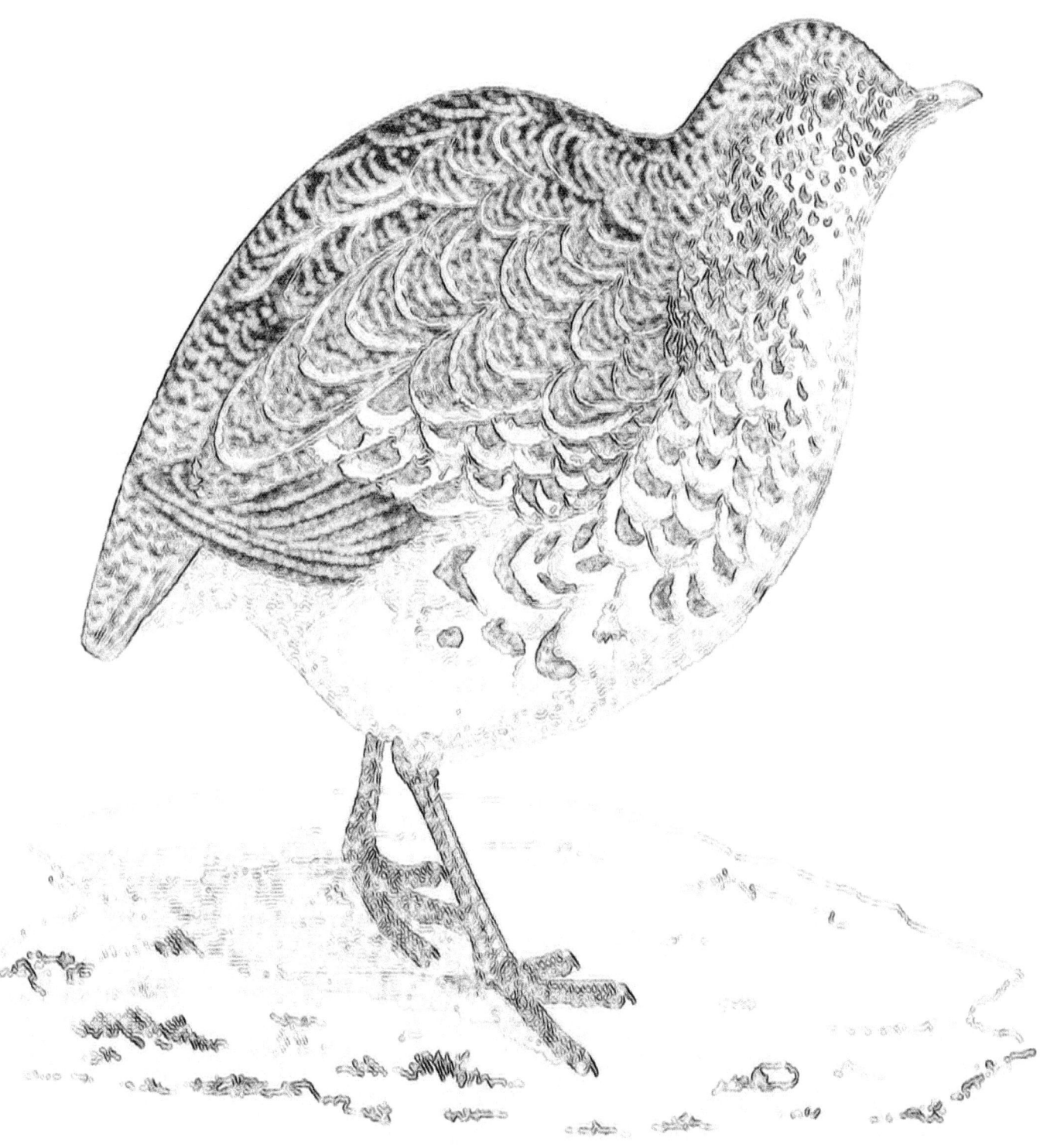

AQUATIC WARBLER

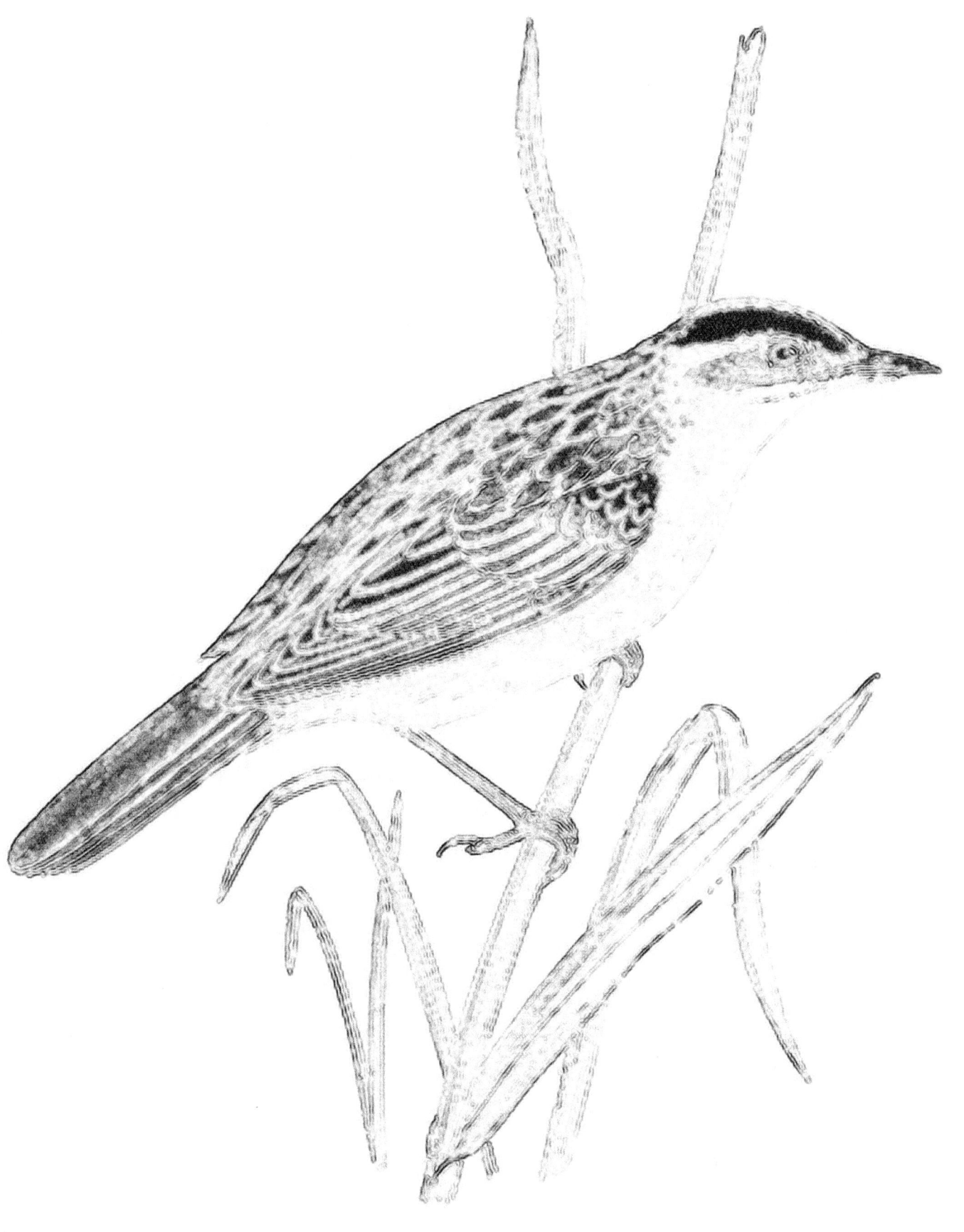

ARCTIC TERN

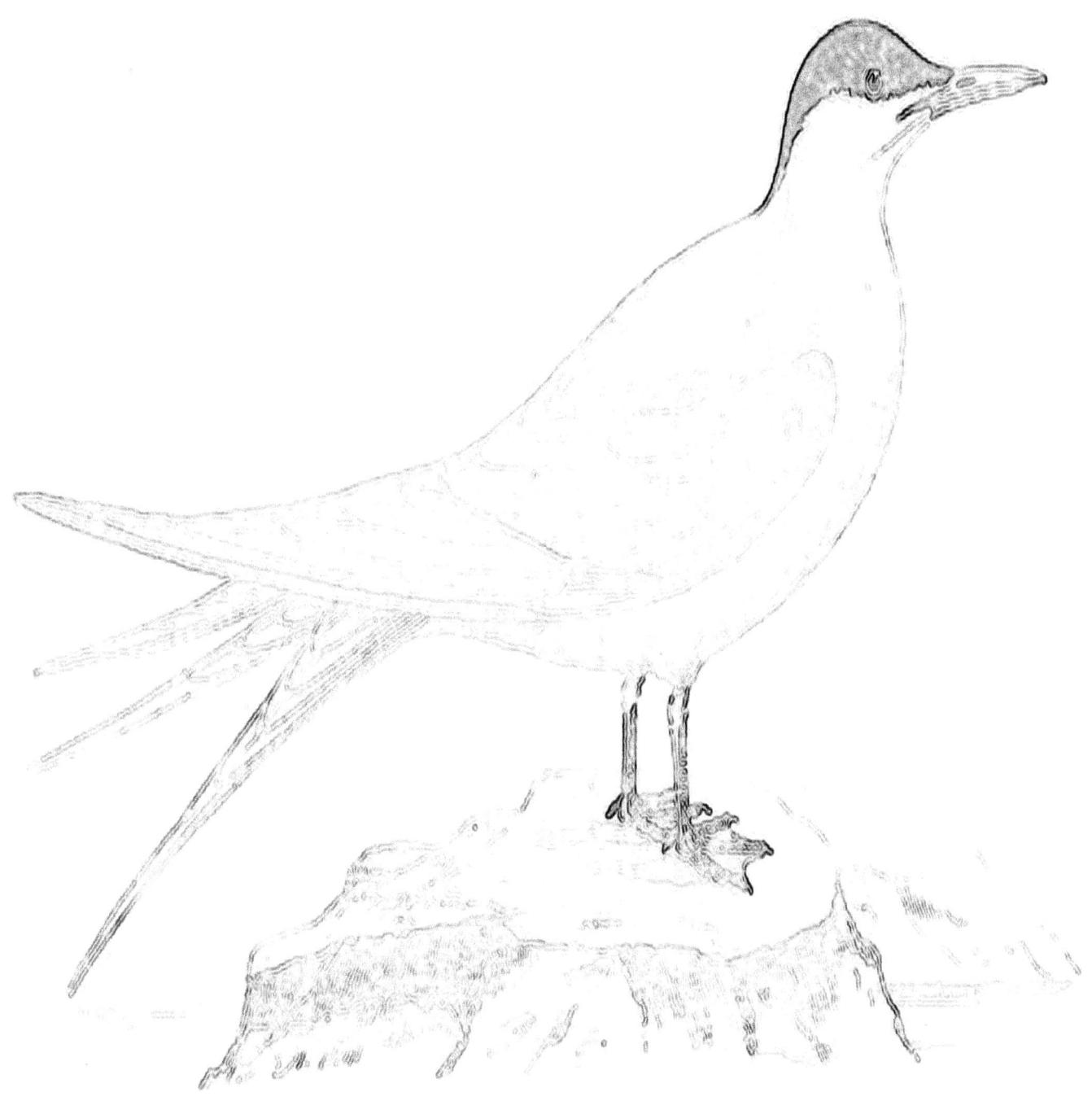

AVOCET

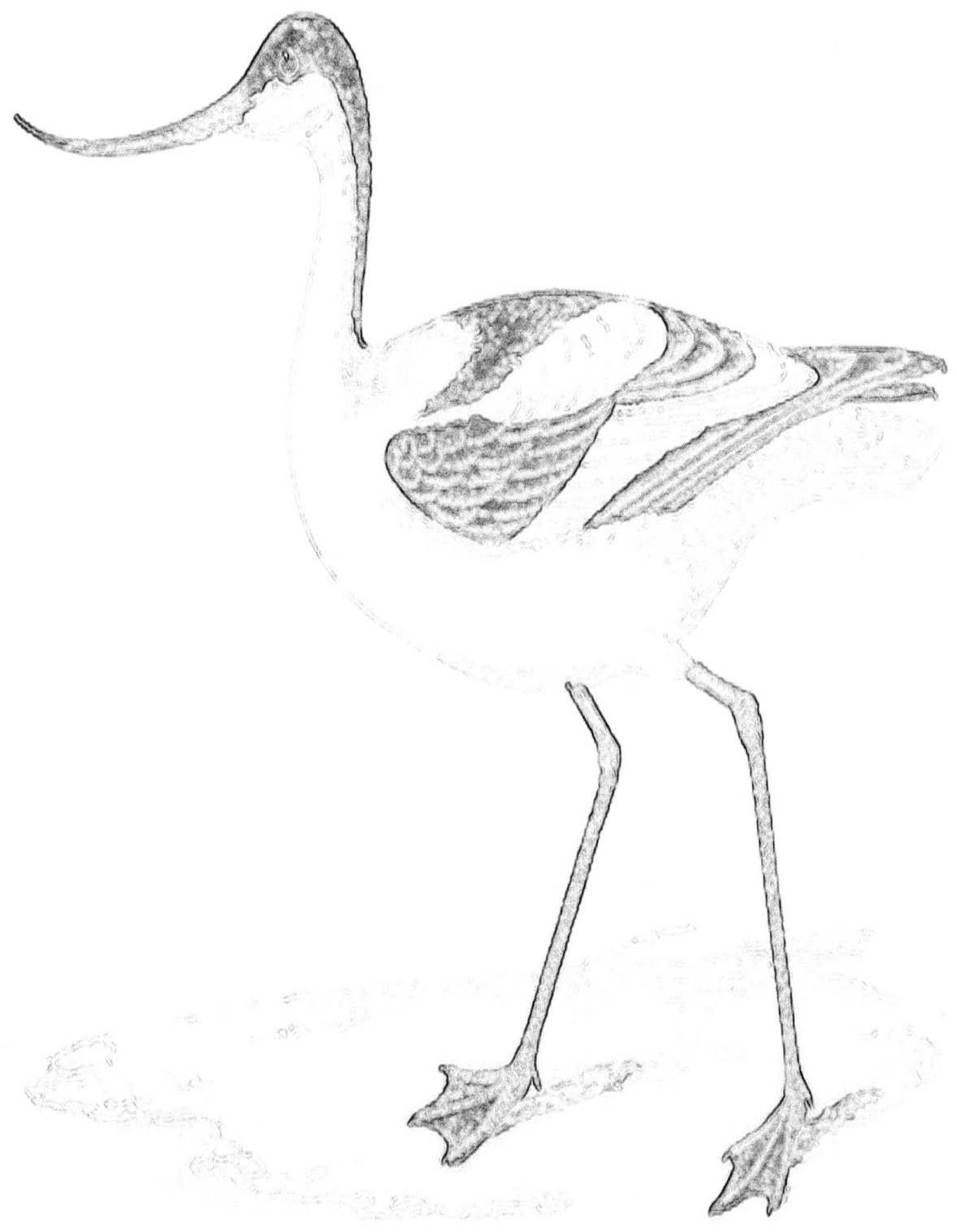

BALTIMORE ORIOLES

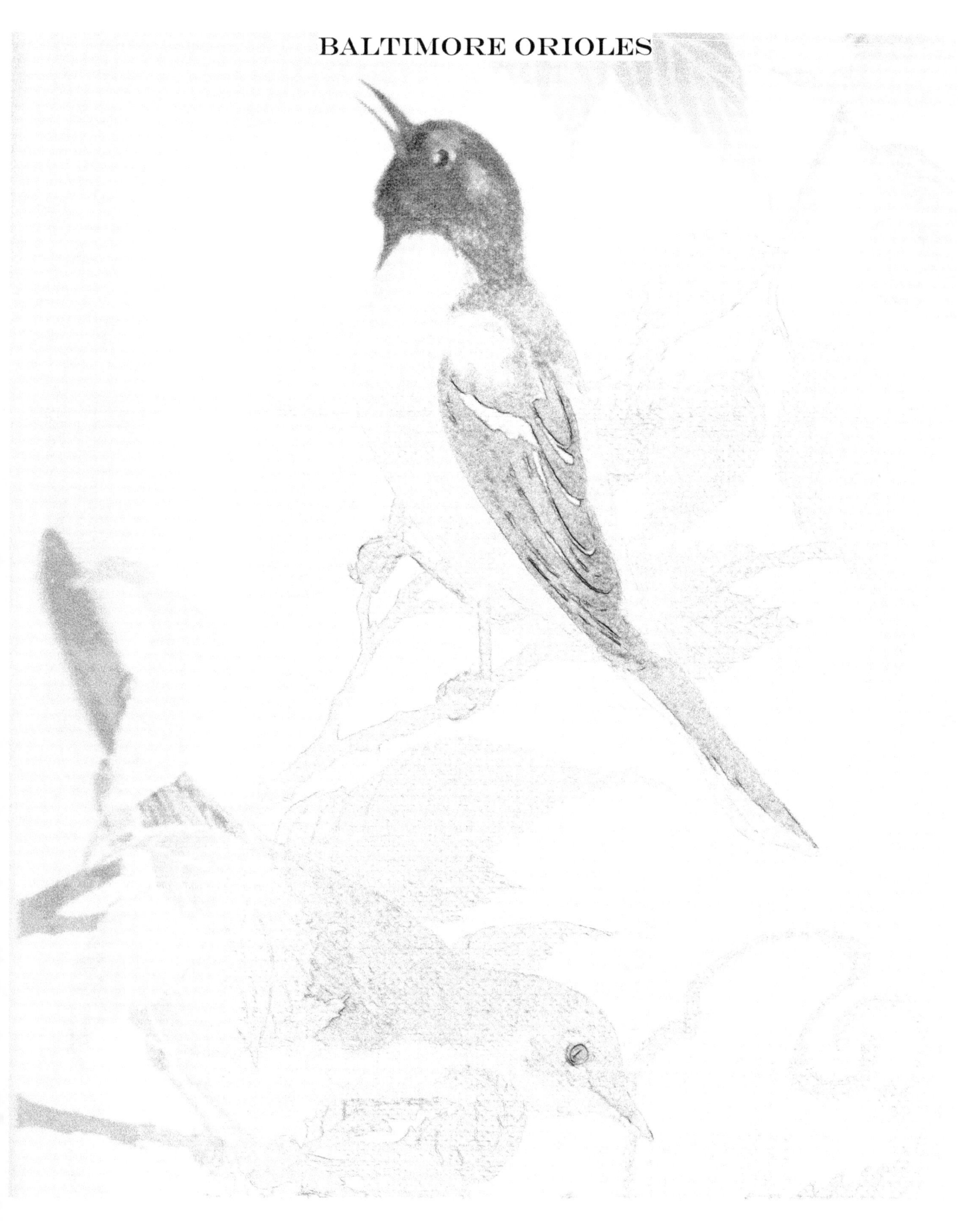

BARN SWALLOW

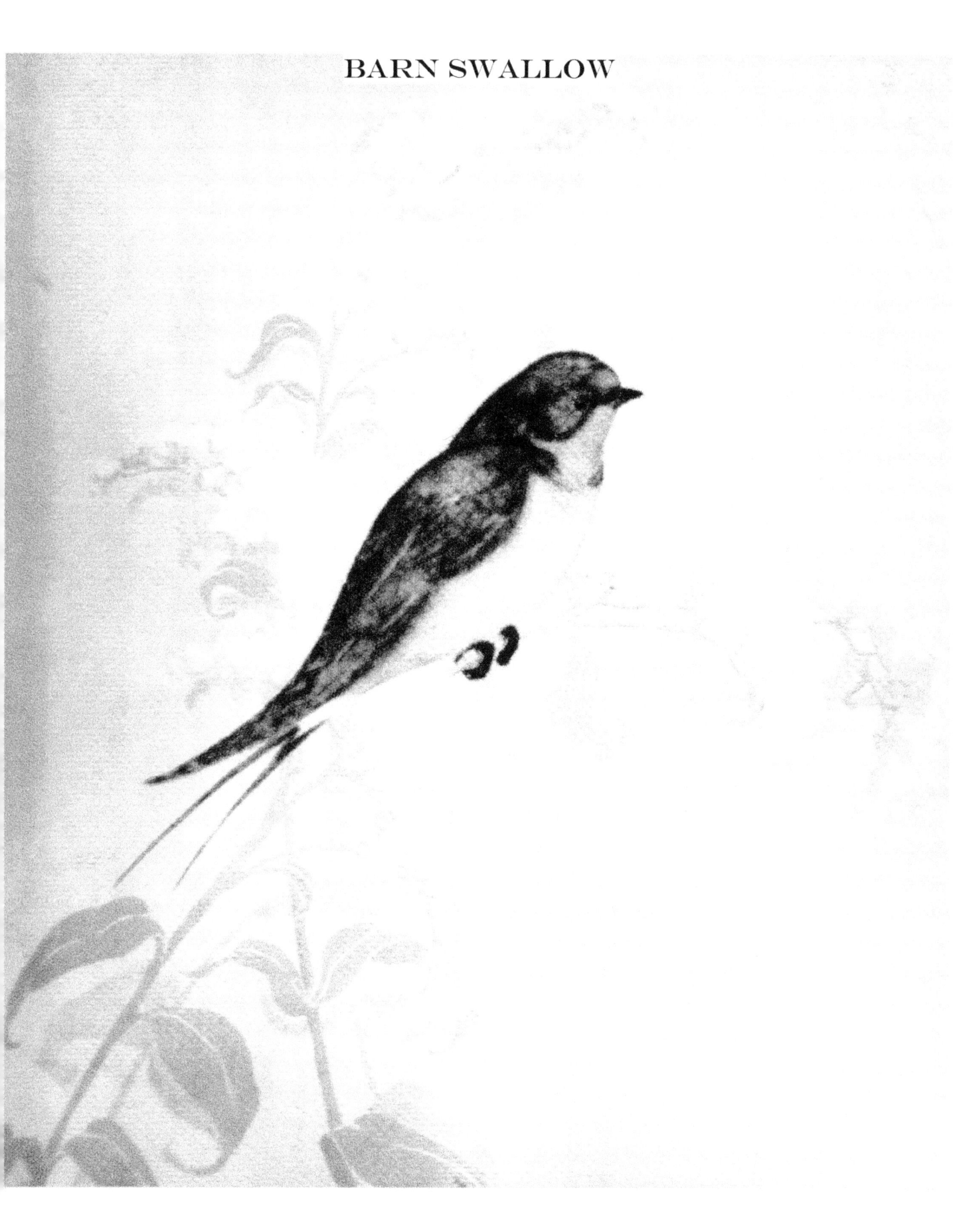

BARRED WARBLER

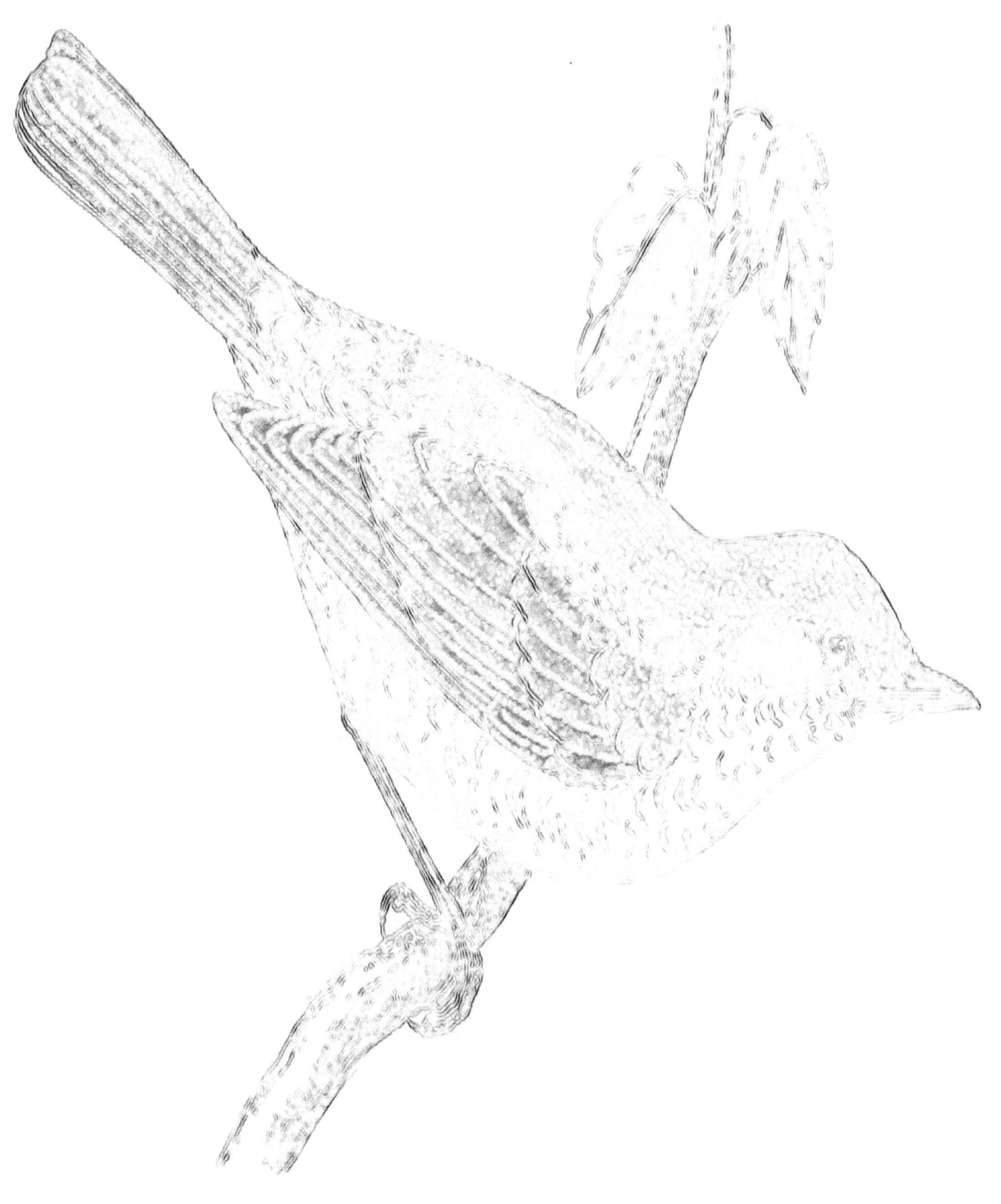

BAR-TAILED GODWIT

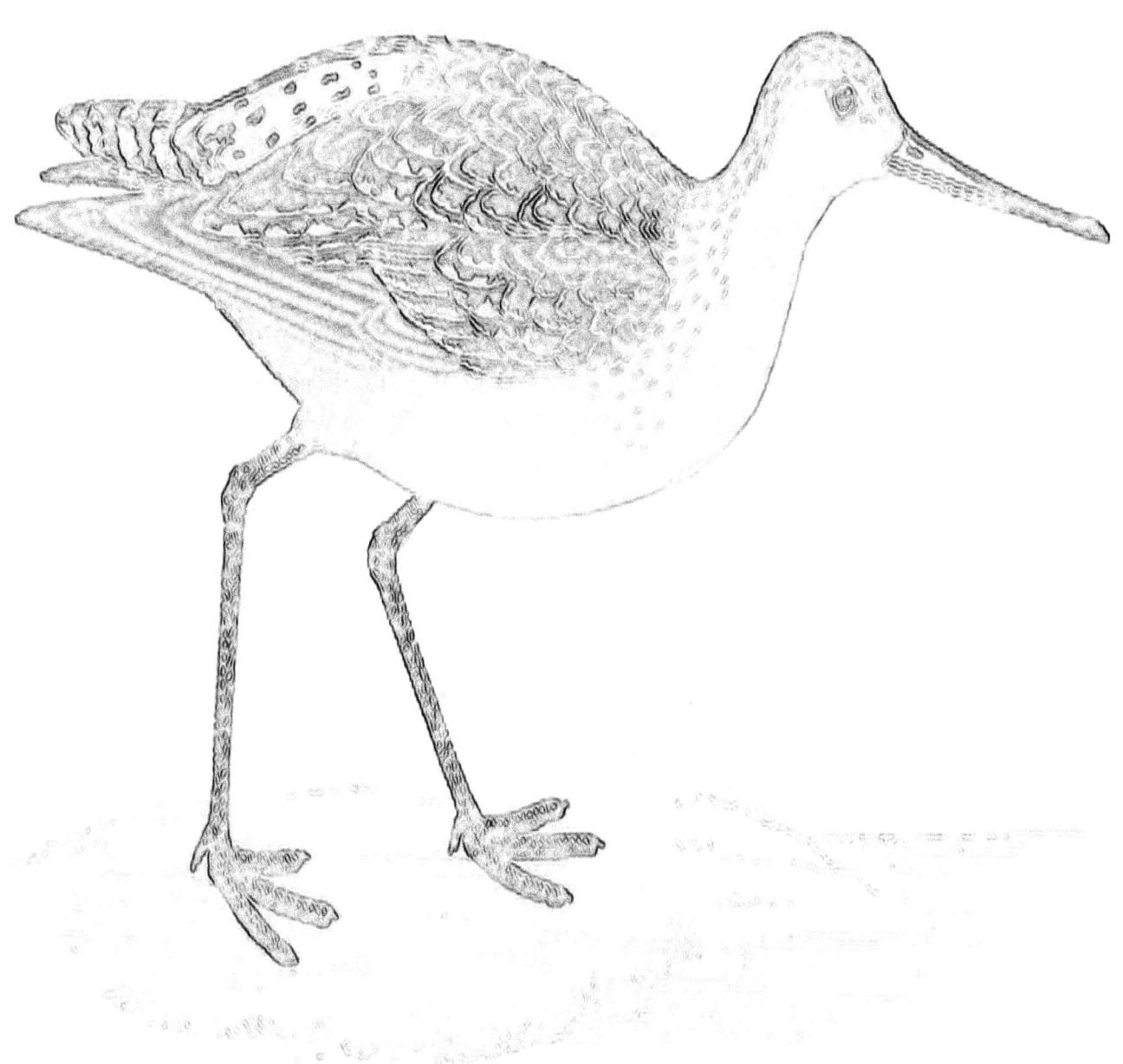

BEAN GOOSE

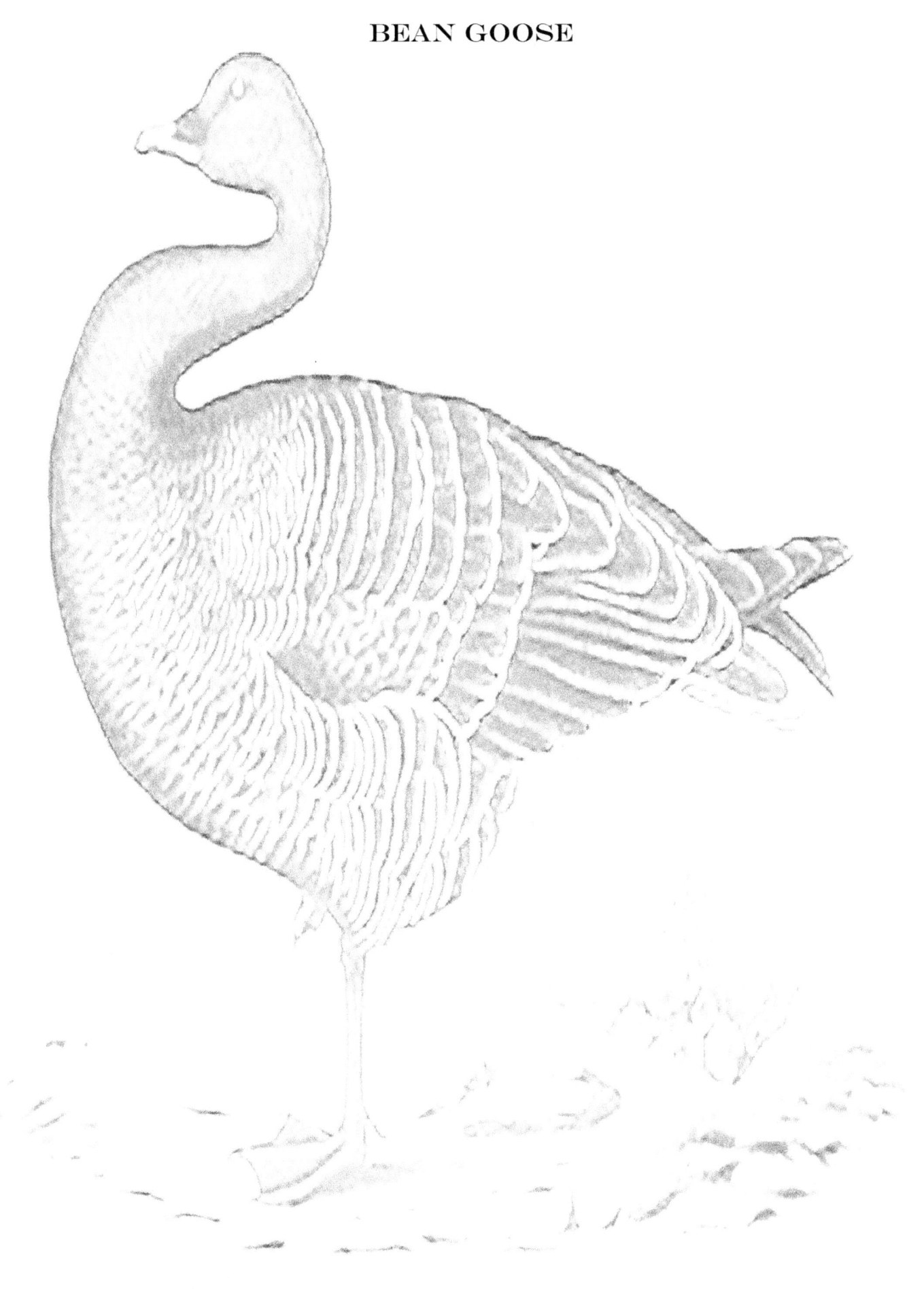

BEARDED TITMOUSE

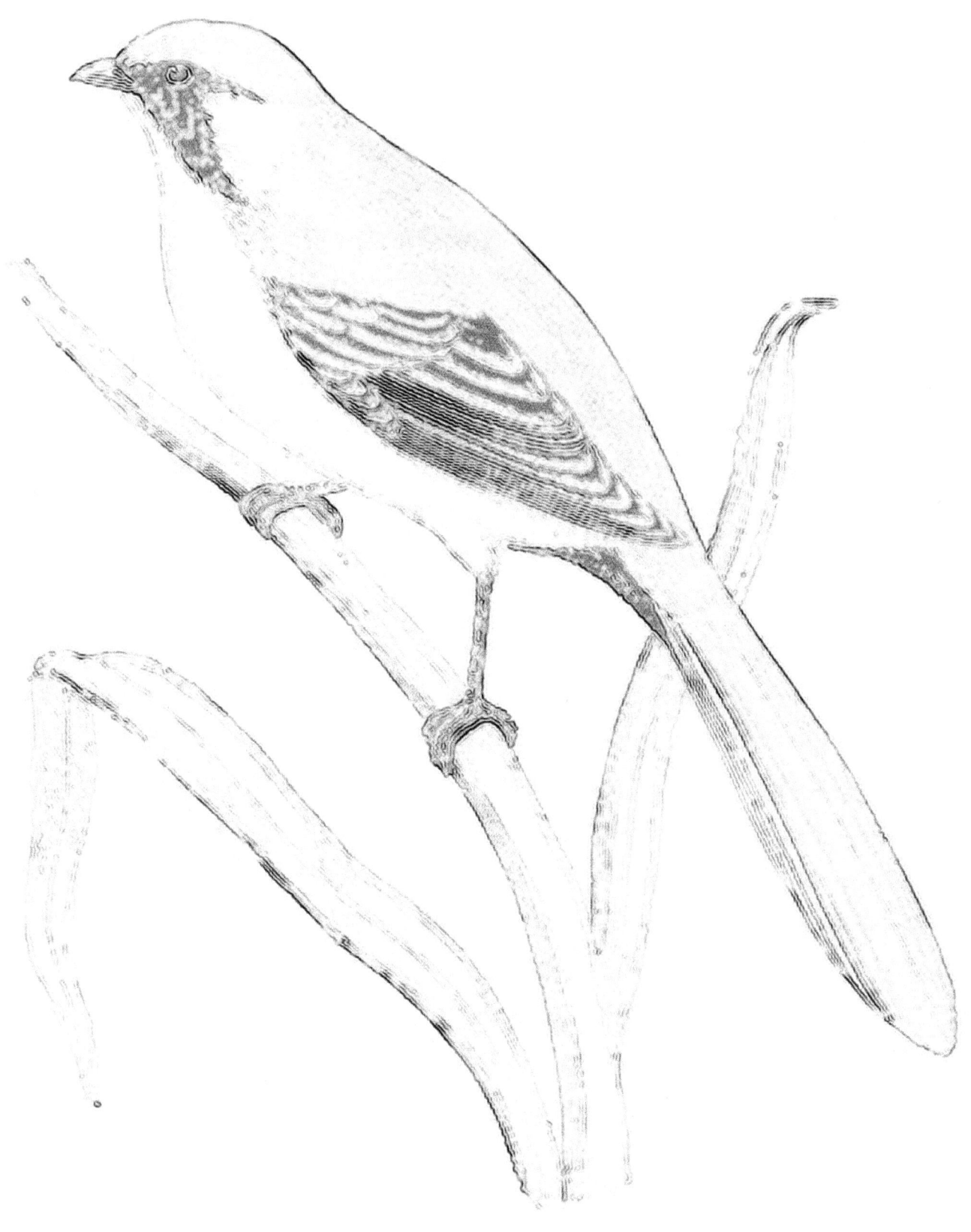

BLACK WINGED STILT

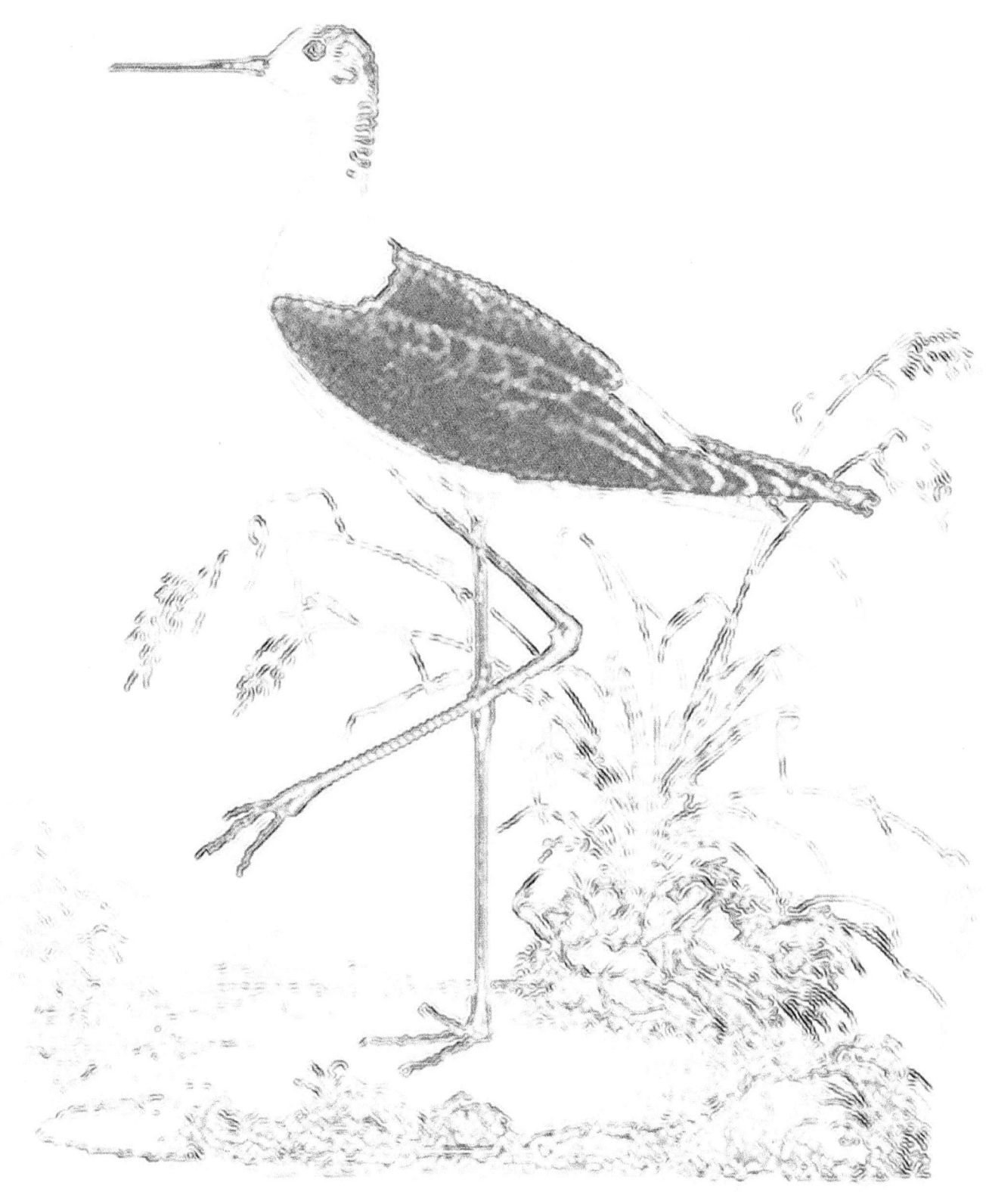

BLUE JAY

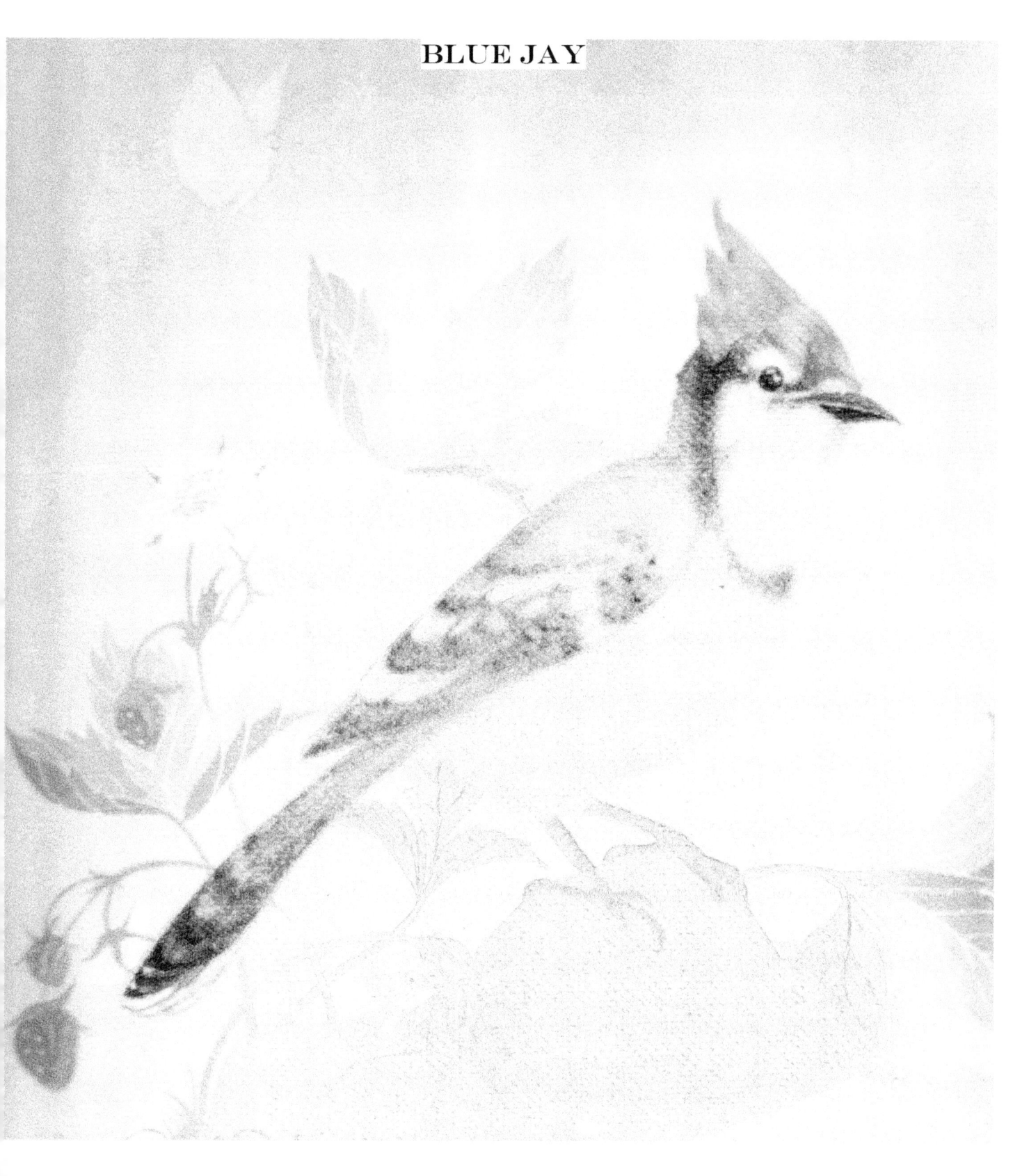

BOBOLINKS

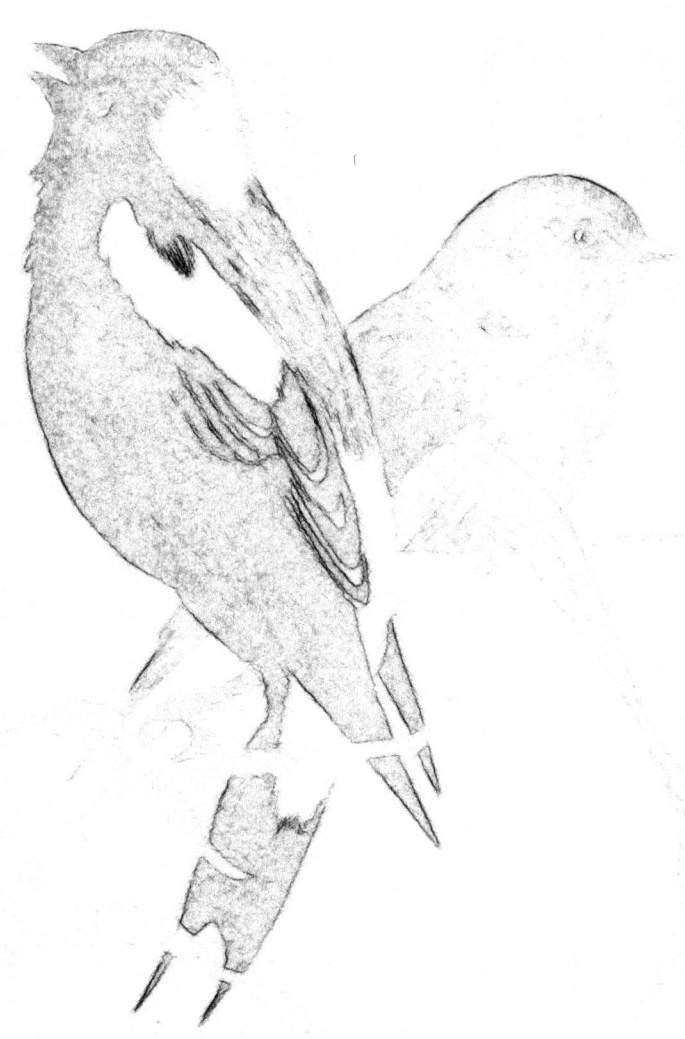

CARDINALS

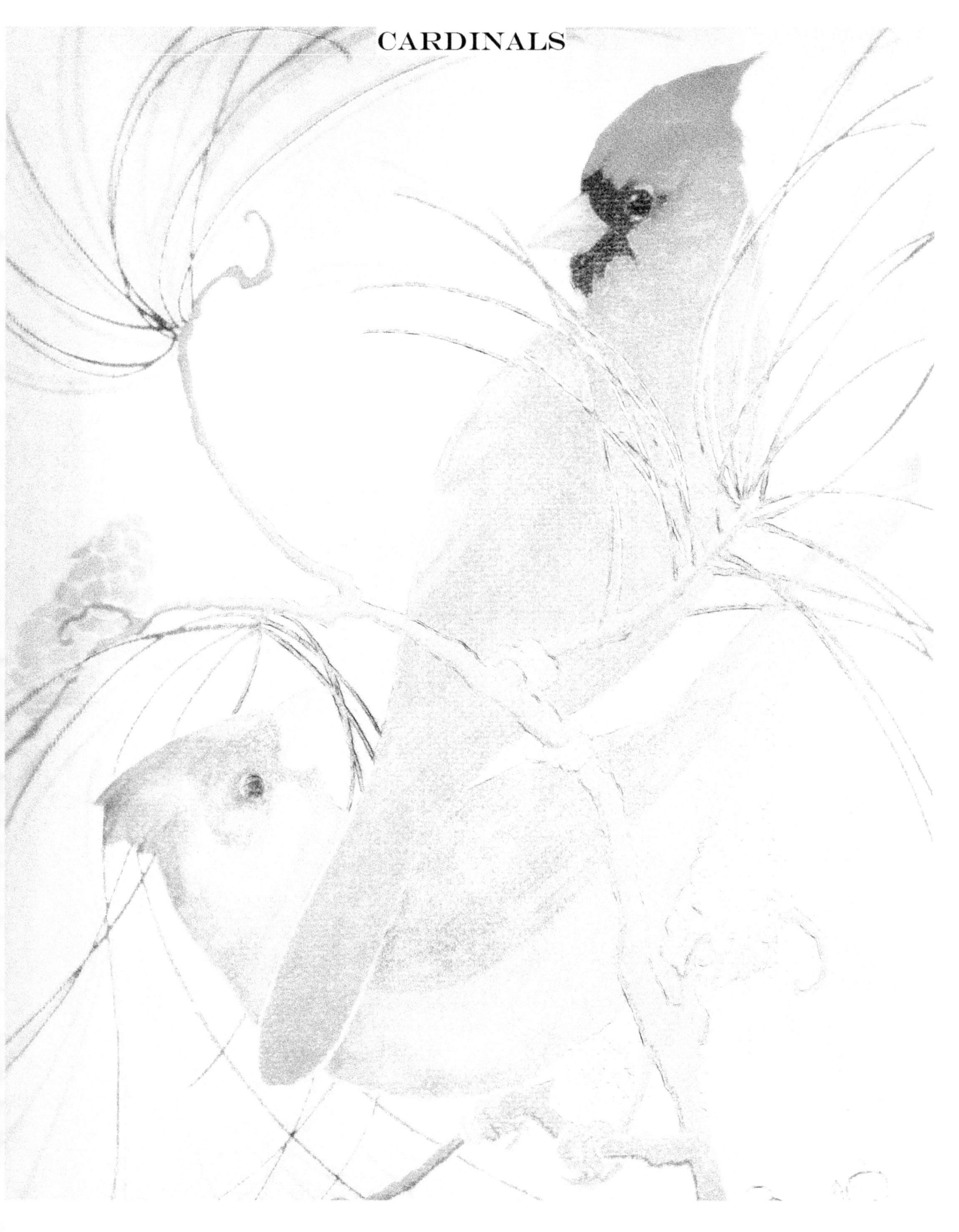

CARDINALS

CREAM COLORED SWIFTFOOT

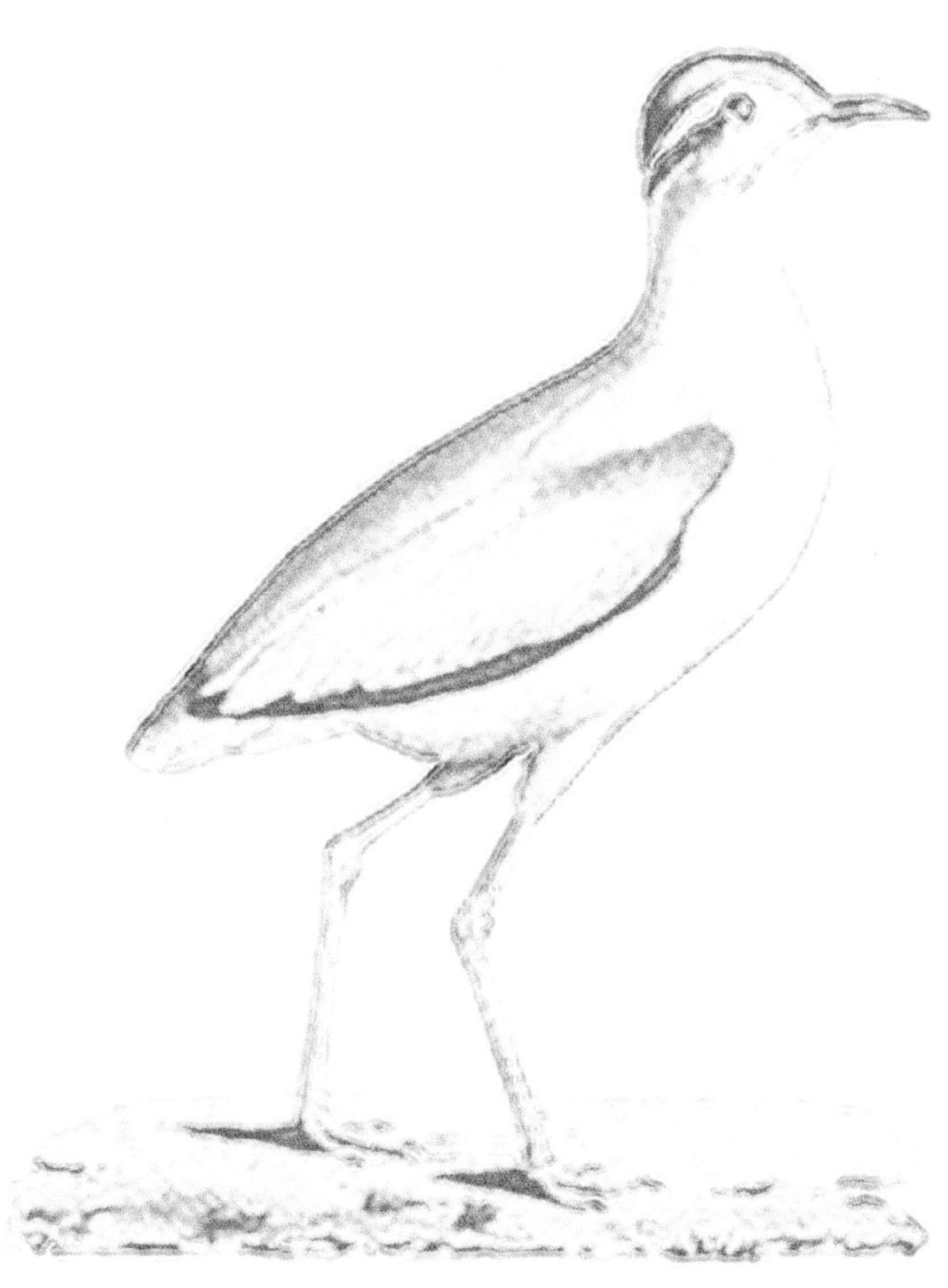

CURLEW

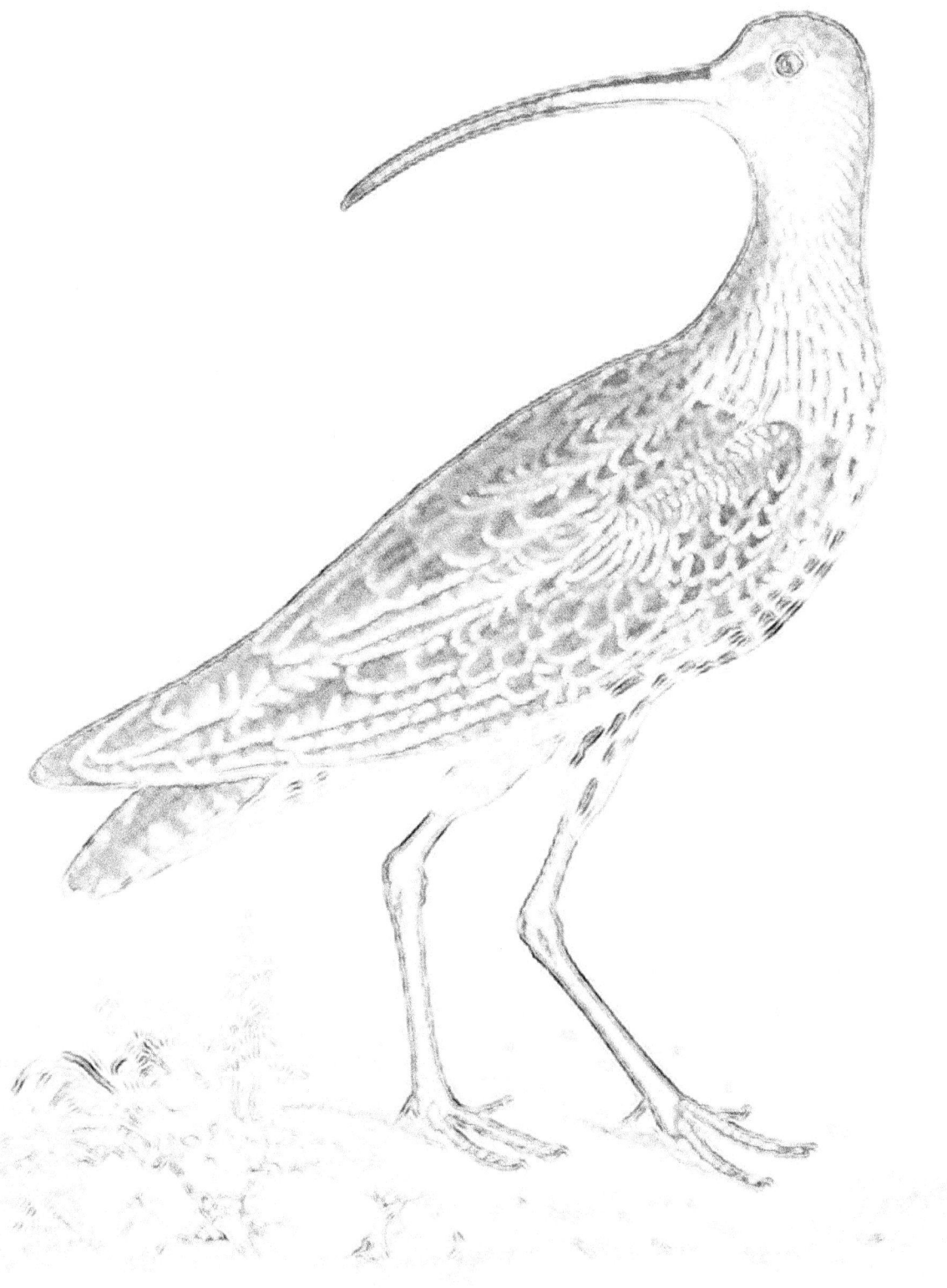

GOOSANDER

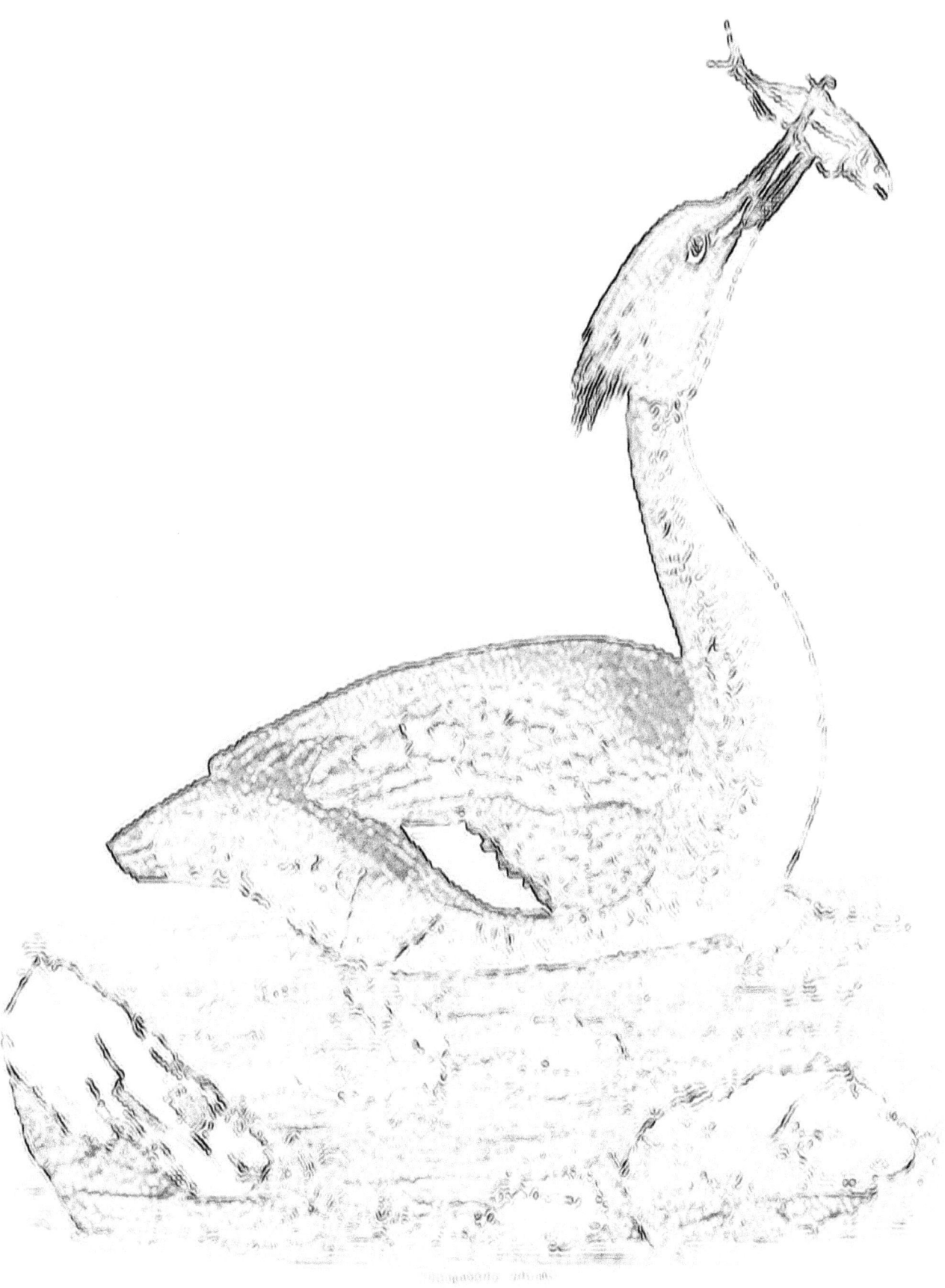

GREY LAPWING

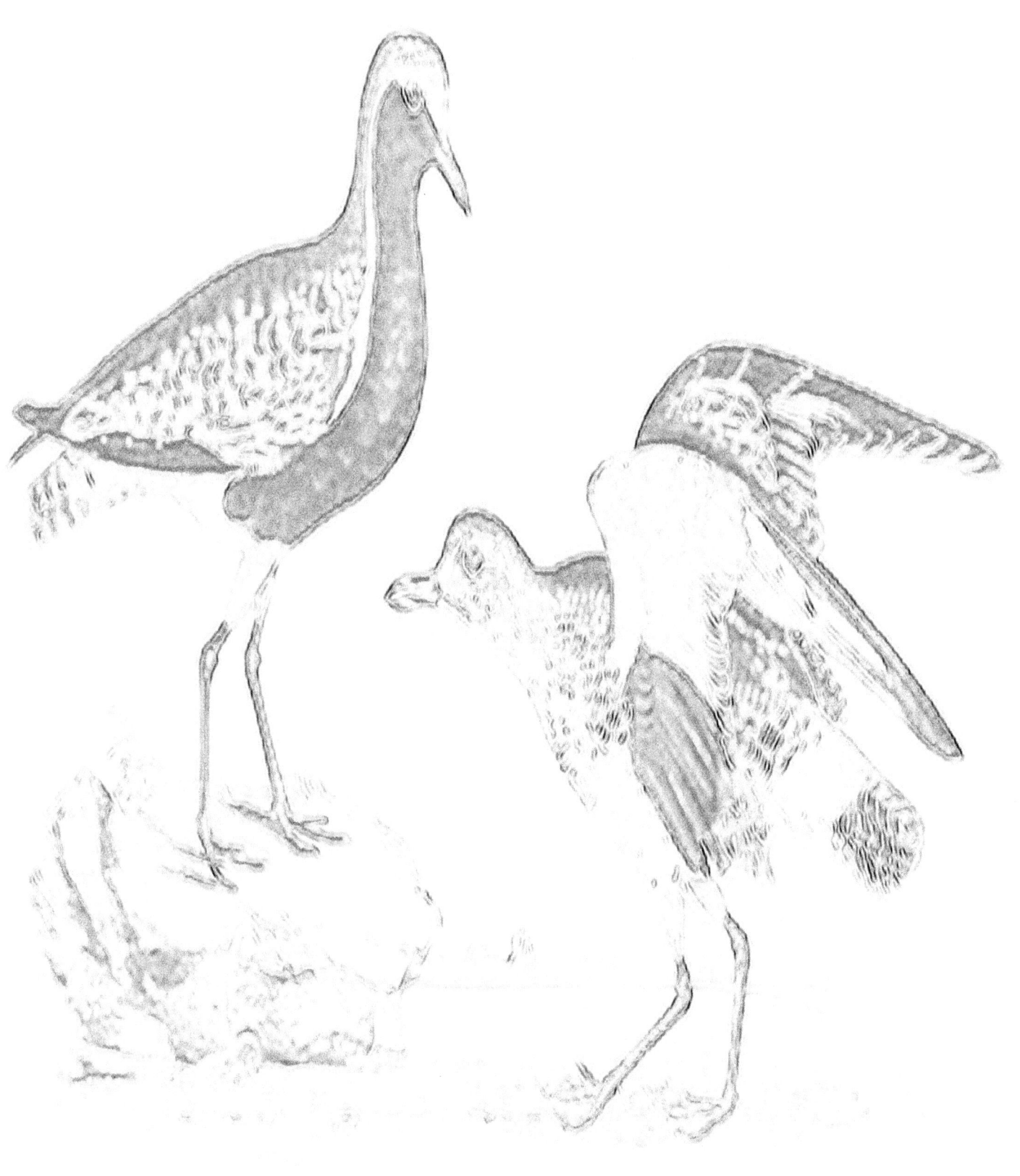

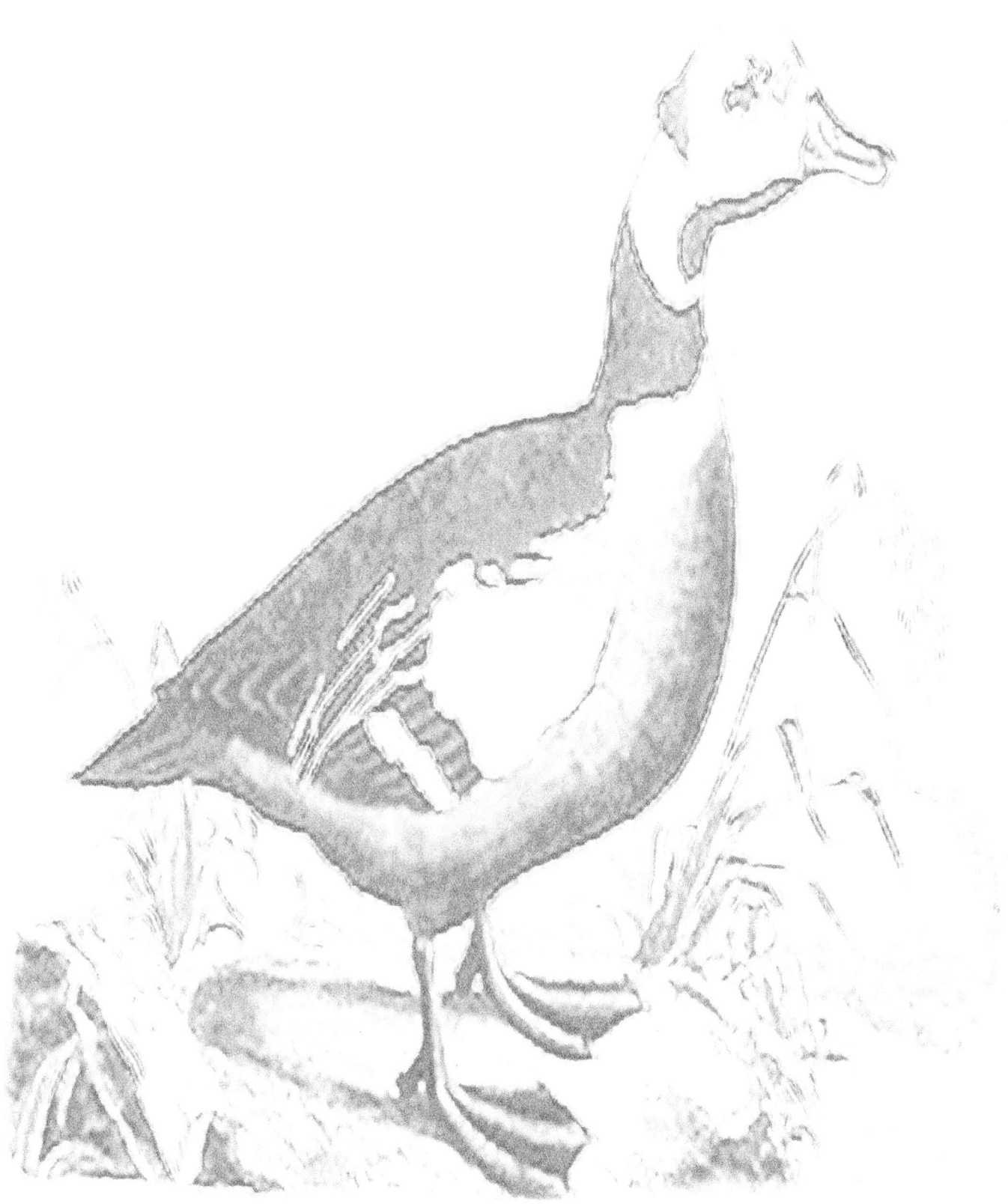

PURPLE HERON

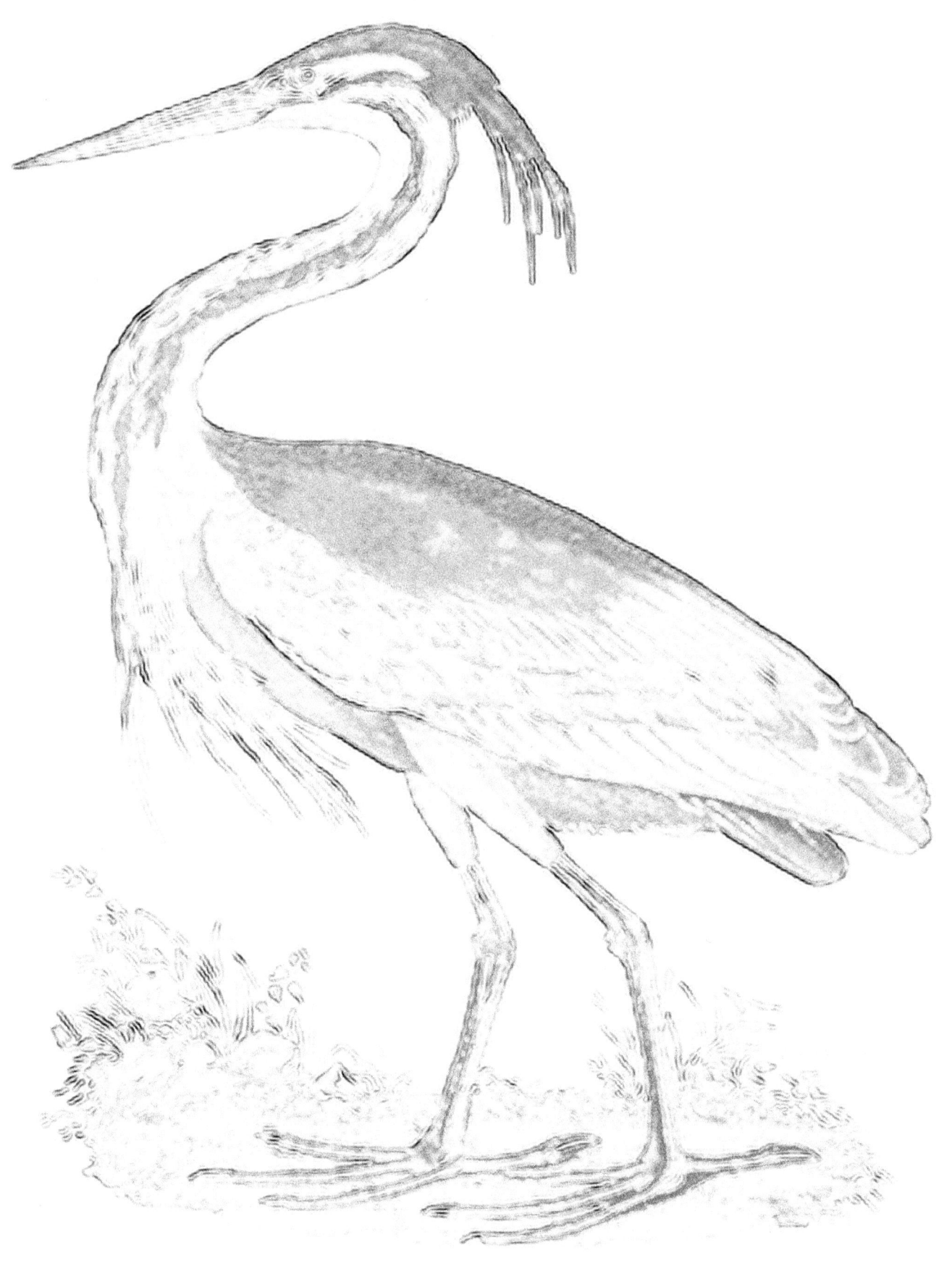

ROBINS

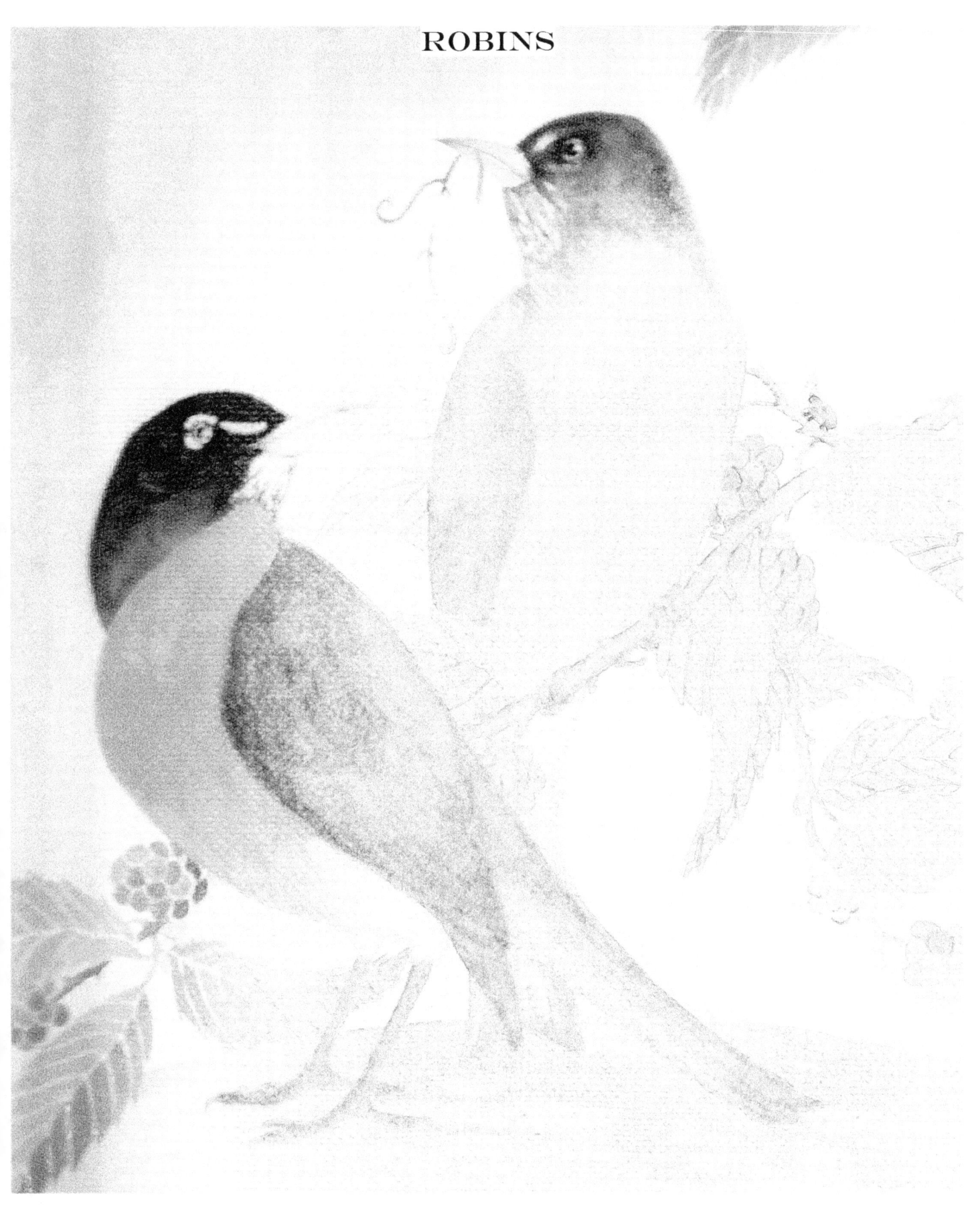

WREN

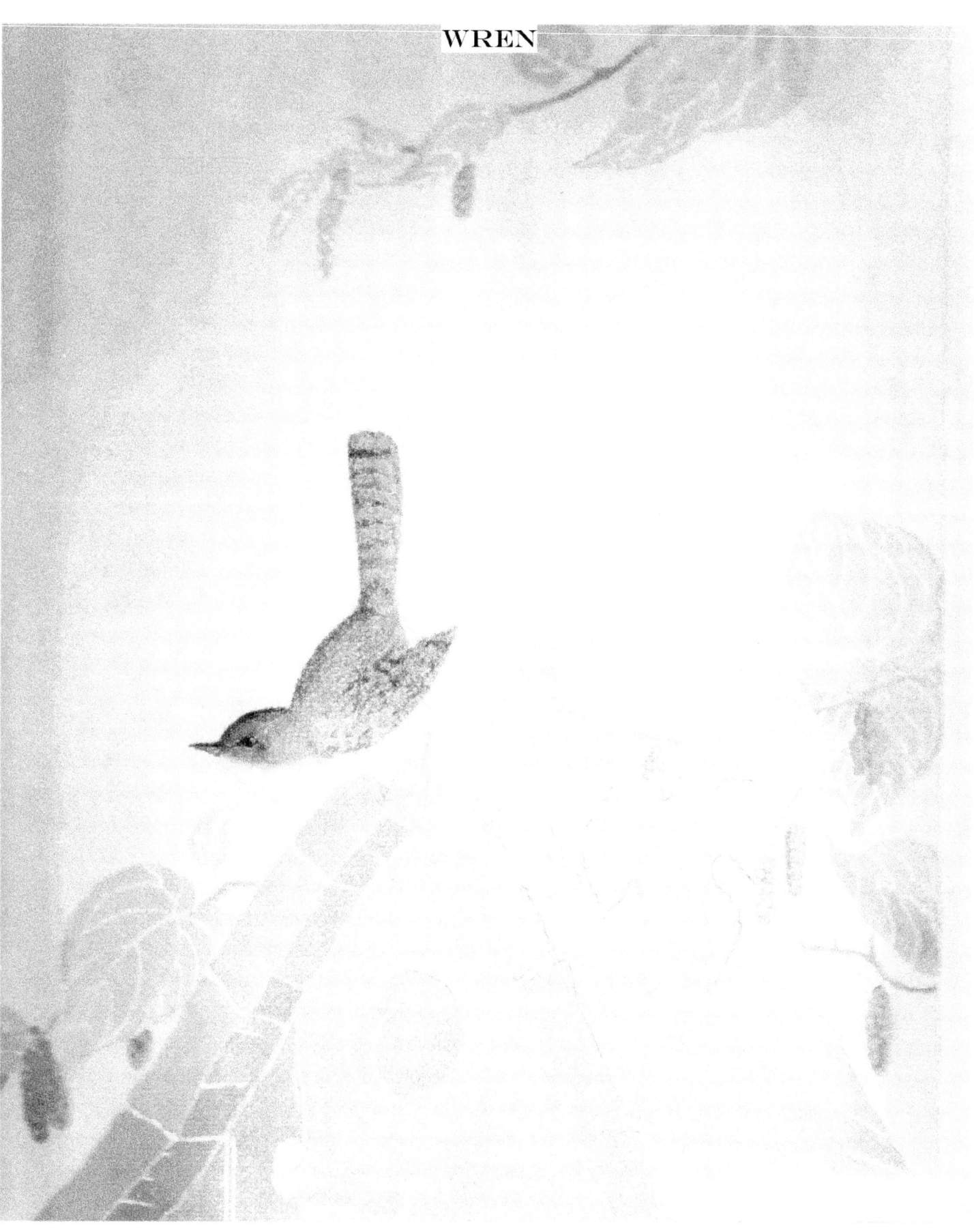